C.H. #12.90

Winston Churchill School
190th & Center
Homewood, IL 60430

From the Library of the
HOMEWOOD PUBLIC SCHOOLS
District No. 153

The world of living things is one of the richest and most fascinating you can explore. This book explains all about life, from simple plants like mosses and ferns, right up to the complex workings of the human eye.

Illustrated with diagrams, cutaway sections and colour pictures, this book will help you understand more about the plants and animals that share the world – and will tempt you to find out even more about living things . . .

Contents

Fungi and Mosses	6
Flowers and Vegetables	8
Trees	10
Unusual Plants	12
Ants and Termites	14
Bees and Wasps	16
Fish	18
Amphibians	20
Reptiles	22
Birds	24
Large and Flightless Birds	26
Rodents	28
Herd Animals and their Predators	30
The Larger Mammals	32
The Big Cats	34
The Polar Regions	36
Monkeys and Apes	38
The Human Body – Flesh and Bone	40
The Major Organs	42
The Five Senses	44
Glossary	46

Larousse

Copyright © MCMLXXXIV by World International Publishing Limited, Great Ducie Street, Manchester, England.
First published in USA by Larousse & Co., Inc., 572 5th Avenue, New York.
ISBN 0-88332-374-5.
Printed in Italy.

Let me tell you about...
LIVING THINGS

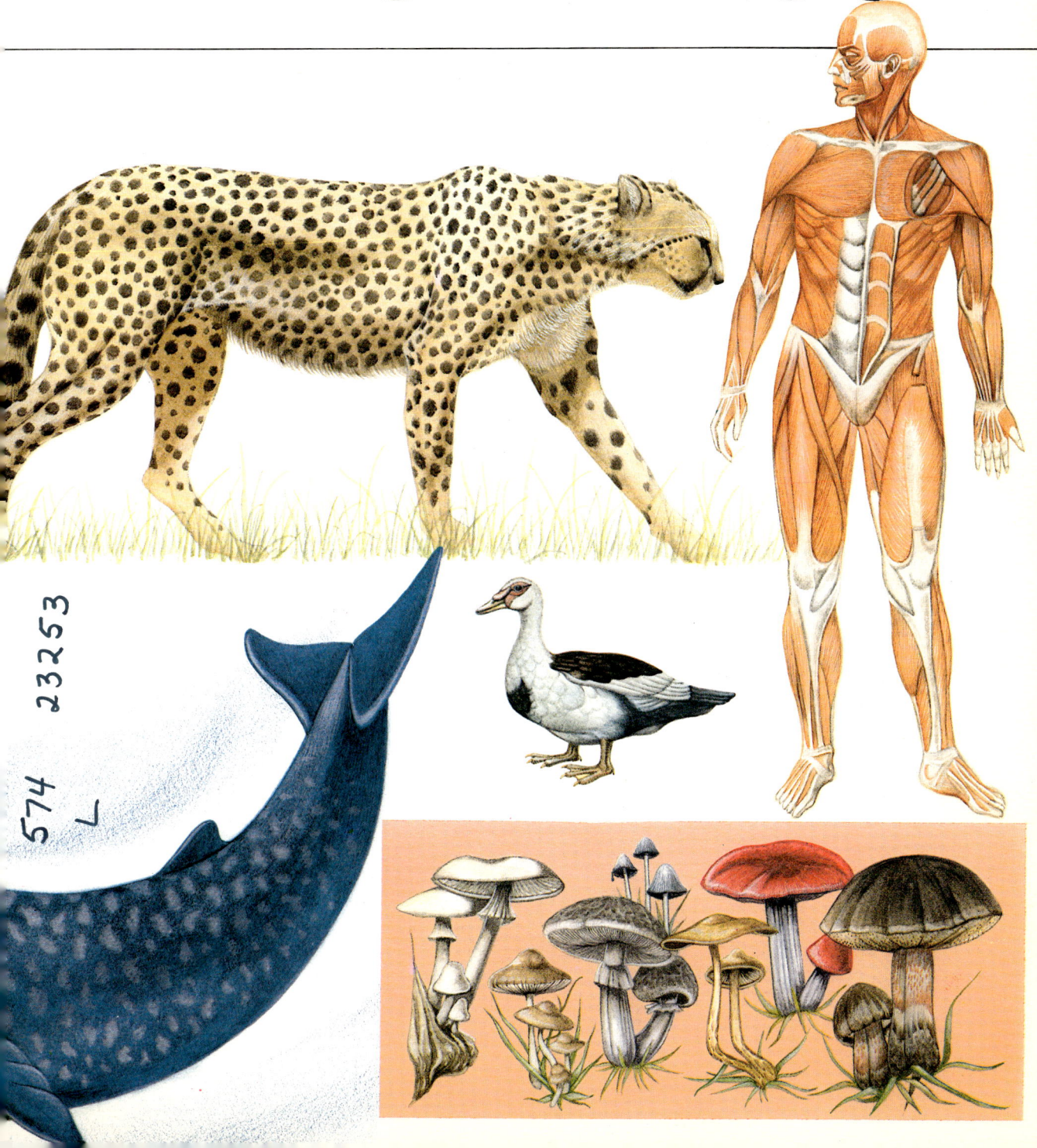

Fungi, Mosses and Ferns

Although they look very unalike, the mushrooms you eat and the greenish mould that grows on stale bread are related to one another; both are *fungi*.

Fungi are plants, but cannot make their own food because they have no *chlorophyll*. (Chlorophyll is the green colour in plants that is essential for them to perform a function called *photosynthesis,* which manufactures the plant's food.) Because of this, fungi must rely on other things for their food supply – usually dead things, stale food and rotting wood – and this is where you are likely to see them.

Unlike flowering plants, fungi do not produce seeds but *spores*. You can see the spores of a mushroom quite clearly, by performing this simple experiment. Take a mushroom and pull off the stalk. Now place the cap down flat on a piece of paper and leave it overnight. In the morning, you will be able to see a pattern like the spokes of a wheel on the paper – the brownish substance making the pattern are thousands of spores that the mushroom makes in its pinkish-brown *gills*.

Because so many toadstools and mushrooms look alike, and because so many are poisonous, it is *very* unwise indeed to eat *any* fungus that you collect from the wild. If you can, wear old gloves if you are going fungus collecting, but if not, remember to wash your hands as soon as possible afterwards.

Mosses and Ferns

Mosses are also flowerless plants, but unlike fungi they can photosynthesise and produce their own food. Their similarity to fungi lies in the fact that they produce spores, not seeds. Mosses do not have proper roots like flowering plants, but tiny rootlets which keep the plant in place. This means that soil is not essential to mosses, and indeed you can often see them growing in 'cushions' on stones and walls.

Ferns are often to be found in warm, damp places, and are also spore-producing. Some of them have leaves which are folded round when they first break through the soil, and then unfurl as the plant grows. The spore-cases are found on the undersides of the leaves, which contain chlorophyll and therefore can photosynthesise.

Flowers and Vegetables

Why Do Plants Have Flowers?

Many flowers are brightly coloured and perfumed, but this is not just for display purposes. The colours and the scents are designed to help *pollinate* the plant's seeds.

Look at the diagram of the flower. At the top of the stalk is a swelling. This is the female part of the flower where the seeds are stored. Around the outside of this you can see thin stalks called *stamens*, which have *anthers* on the ends. These are the male parts of the flower, and the pollen of the flower is found here. To ensure that the plant's seeds will grow, pollen from the anthers has to join with the seeds – and this is where the action of insects comes in.

In order to attract the insects which can carry the pollen from one flower to another, the plant will very often have brightly – coloured or scented petals, and in addition will manufacture *nectar* which most insects will come in search of. As the insect lands on the flower and crawls to reach the nectar, it brushes against the pollen-bearing anthers, collecting it on its back or legs as it does so. You can often see bees flying about in summer with a dusting of yellow pollen on their furry bodies.

If you have ever watched a bee or butterfly in the garden, you will have noticed that it visits not one, but many flowers. In this way, you can be sure that as it picks up pollen from one plant, it is also depositing pollen on that same flower, ensuring that the seeds are pollinated.

The flower petals soon die and drop, leaving the seed box, with its fertilised seeds inside it. Every plant has a different way of dispersing its seeds, and a good many of them are blown away in the breeze – dandelions are one example of this. But some of them become the centre of the fruit of their plant, like apples or tomatoes.

If you cut an apple in half, from top to bottom, you will be able to see the seeds of the apple tree inside the fruit. The edible part of the apple itself is composed of the seed box of the flower, which swelled to protect the seeds until they could reach the ground and grow.

Some seeds can be very large indeed – for example, a coconut is a seed – but many are quite small. Some orchid seeds are so small that you would see them as fine dust, and others are, like ash-keys, so common that we barely notice them, or even think of them as seeds.

What is a vegetable?

Basically, any part of a plant that we eat that isn't a fruit – it's as simple as that! Many vegetables are grown specifically as food for humans or animals, and can be any part of a certain plant. For example, the potato is what is called a *tuber*, and grows on the root of the potato plant, while a pea is a seed and yet is called a vegetable. Parsnips and turnips are also roots, but beansprouts are the stalks of their plants. Tomatoes, on the other hand, are fruits, as they contain their seeds, which you can see every time you cut a tomato in half.

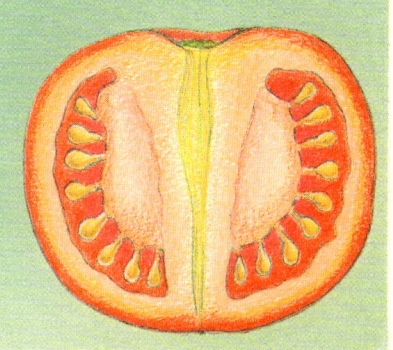

Trees

Although they may not look very similar, trees have a great resemblance to small flowering plants, in that they have flowers, and produce seeds. The seeds might not be easily recognisable as such, since many of them are large – for example, the coconut and the horse chestnut (conker) – but they perform the same function as the seeds of smaller plants.

Trees are very much larger than other plants – the Californian Redwood, for example, reaches heights of more than 250 feet (83 metres), with an average trunk width of 12 feet (4 metres) – and round their trunks they have a layer of *bark*, spongy but tough material which protects the living wood from injury. Some trees are grown commercially for something they produce – the sap of the rubber tree, for example, is used to make rubber, and the cork oak's bark is, not surprisingly, used as cork.

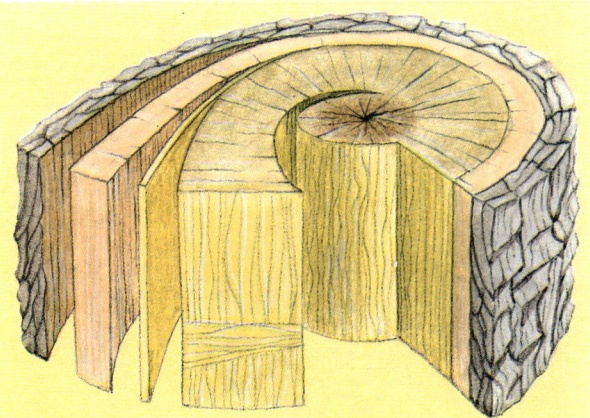

The Wood Inside the Tree

The trunk of the tree is made up of a number of layers, each with its special function to perform.

Water is pulled up through the *xylem* cells from the roots by evaporation from the leaves. Food made by the leaves by photosynthesis is carried by the *phloem* cells from the leaves to all parts of the tree, while the *cambium* cells build a new layer of wood round the trunk every year, making the rings which can be seen when the tree is cut down.

To Shed or Not to Shed

As you know, many trees lose their leaves in the autumn and remain bare until the warmer, brighter weather of spring. These are known as *deciduous* trees, while the ones which retain their leaves are called *evergreens*. Looking carefully at one sort of each tree, it is easy to see why they behave as they do.

The Deciduous Sycamore

The sycamore's leaves, as you can see, are broad and flat in order to catch the sunlight for photosynthesis. During the short, dark days of autumn and winter, there would be little sunlight, and so the green chlorophyll decomposes and the true colours of the leaf – the yellows and reds – begin to show through. The tree 'shuts down' for the cold months, but because the leaves are still losing much more water than the tree can afford (they do this because of the broad surfaces of the leaves, each covered in pores which give out water) the tree has to shed the leaves altogether.

The Evergreen Pine

The pine tree does not have broad leaves like the sycamore. Instead it has thin needle-like leaves, each one covered in a waxy layer of *cutin*, a substance which greatly slows down the evaporation of water from the pores of a leaf. This means that although the leaf of the pine does not need as much sunlight as that of a sycamore, it can carry on photosynthesising all through the cold, dark winter days too, and so there is no need for the tree to shed its leaves. Cutin is found on the leaves of the holly, too, which, although it has a broad leaf, is not a deciduous plant for this very reason.

Plants How green plants make their food

The green colour of plants is caused by a substance in their tissue called *chlorophyll*, and this is vital to the life of the plant, as without it *photosynthesis* could not take place.

Photosynthesis is the process whereby green plants take elements present all around them and process them into food for themselves. These elements are carbon dioxide (CO_2) from the air, water (H_2O) from the soil, sunlight, and chlorophyll, which is present in the leaves of the plant. By a chemical process, the plant converts these elements into a sugary starch on which it feeds. It is only possible to do this in the part of the plant which contains chlorophyll. In plants which have *variegated* or two-coloured leaves, it is the green part only which produces the starch. Plants which have no chlorophyll at all must rely on some other source for their food, like the fungi. These are called *parasitic* plants.

Mistletoe is semi-parasitic, as it contains chlorophyll in its leaves and therefore can manufacture its own food. However, it does rely on its host for certain materials it is unable to make for itself.

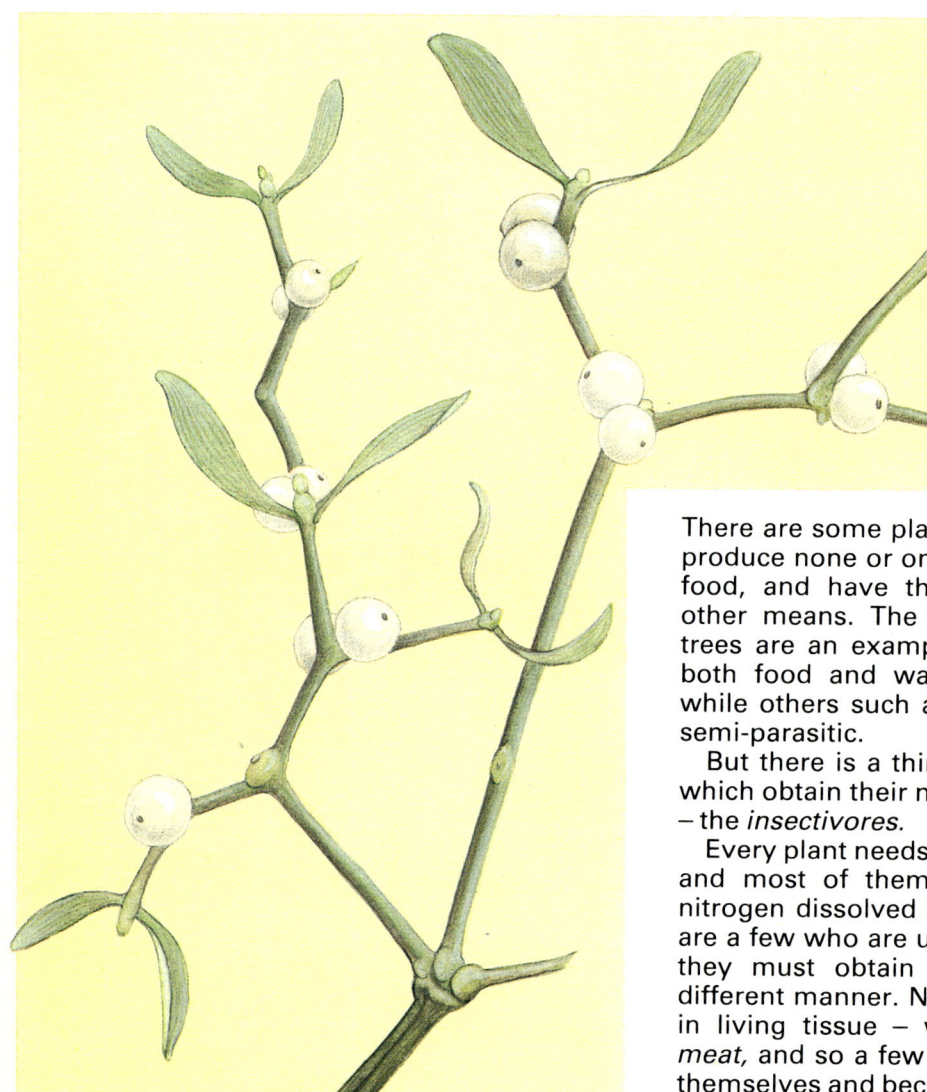

There are some plants which are able to produce none or only some of their own food, and have therefore to resort to other means. The fungi which live on trees are an example of this, obtaining both food and water from their host, while others such as mistletoe are only semi-parasitic.

But there is a third category of plants which obtain their needs by other means – the *insectivores*.

Every plant needs a supply of nitrogen, and most of them obtain it from the nitrogen dissolved in the soil. But there are a few who are unable to do this, and they must obtain their nitrogen in a different manner. Nitrogen is also found in living tissue – what we would call *meat,* and so a few plants have adapted themselves and become fly-catchers.

The best-known of these plants is probably the *Venus' fly-trap*. This has leaves with two lobes at the end, both of which lie flat, like an open book.
Around the outside of the two lobes there are spikes, which when the leaf closes interlock with each other. On the flat surface of the lobes, there are three *trigger hairs.* When an insect or anything else touches one of these hairs, the leaf snaps shut, trapping whatever it has caught inside. If it is an insect, the plant digests the 'meaty' part of it and opens up again to release the skin – if the captive is a twig or a leaf, then the lobes will open again fairly quickly.

Another insectivorous plant which catches its prey a little differently is the *sundew*. Unlike the Venus' fly-trap, the sundew's leaves themselves do not move, but they have red hairs on them which do. Each hair has tiny beads of a sticky fluid on its tip. When a small insect lands on the leaf or walks on it, it gets stuck. The red hairs slowly bend over to hold the insect down, and then the plant can dissolve the insect and absorb the parts it uses. Finally, the hard parts, the wings and skin, blow away in the wind.

A third kind of insectivorous plant is the *pitcher plant* found in the tropics. This is shaped like a large cup or pitcher, and can be a variety of colours to attract its prey. Inside the pitcher the walls are very slippery, and the rim of the cup has stiff, down-pointed hairs on it, to prevent the insect crawling out. Generally the prey slips down into a pool of liquid at the base of the pitcher. This digests the insect, and the pitcher plant receives the nourishment it needs.

Like other plants, the insectivores need to attract insects to them, and so they have developed bright colours to draw attention to themselves, and in some cases smells too. For this reason, the insectivores tend to be dull red and green, as these seem to be the two colours most attractive to their prey.

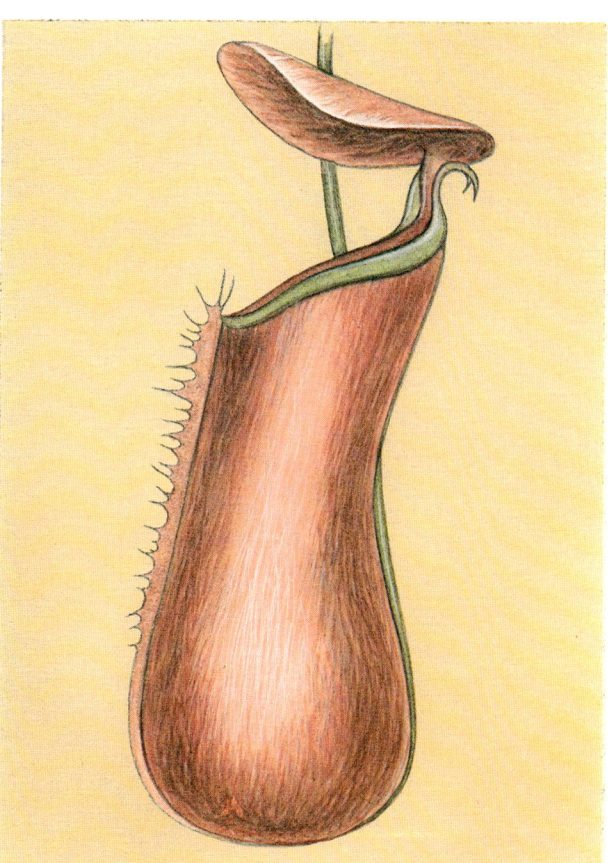

Ants and Termites

Although many people think that ants and termites are closely related, they are not. Apart from the fact that they are both very small and both live in colonies, they have very little in common with each other.

Ants

Ants are far higher up the evolutionary scale than termites. They have a rigid class or *caste* system within the nest. The *queen* is the most important, as it is her job to lay eggs. She does this non-stop until she dies, and is tended by *workers*. These are undeveloped females, and as their name suggests they do all the work in the colony. Each one has a particular job to do – to repair and guard the nest, to gather food, to tend the queen or to care for the eggs.

Finally there are *drones*, who are present only to mate with the queen and ensure the continuation of the nest. The drones die after mating because, as they do no other work, it would not be practical for them to have food wasted on them.

The ants' nest is made up of a complex series of passages and chambers, each with its own function. It is usually found underground, where most of the ants' food – small insects, earthworms and the *honeydew* (a sweet liquid made by aphids) is found.

Termites

Like ants, termites live in colonies, but these are not necessarily found underground. In fact, certain types of termite in Africa and Australia build huge mounds of soil mixed with their own saliva, some reaching heights of over 20 feet (6 metres).

Again, there are three castes. The first is the *royal* caste. Termites have both a king and a queen, whose job is to produce eggs. They are kept prisoner, and if one should die it is replaced by a *supplementary* king or queen. The *worker* termites, like the ants, do all the tasks of the colony except one, guarding, which is the job of the *soldiers*. Soldier termites are very good guards, but in everything else they are completely helpless, and must be fed and groomed by the workers.

Unlike ants, termites will eat almost anything, including wood and paper, and in some cases even metal. They also do great damage to crops like sugar cane and orange trees.

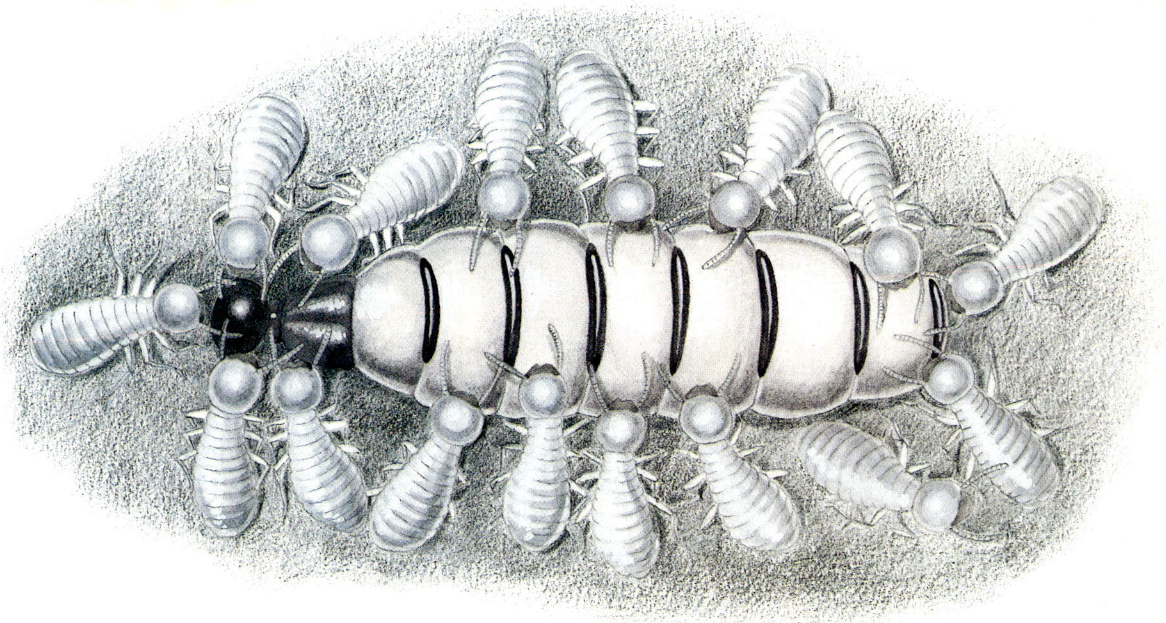

Bees and Wasps

Some insects live in colonies or groups. They are called *social insects,* and one of the best known species of social insect is the honey bee.

Honey bees have been kept by humans for hundreds of years for the honey that they make. Wooden boxes called *hives* are made for them to nest in, and this makes it easier for us to study them and learn about their fascinating lifestyle.

In any hive, the most important inhabitant is the *queen*. She is there to lay the eggs which ensure the continuation of the hive, and that is all she does. The queen is a prolific mother – at certain times she may lay up to fifteen hundred eggs a day, and is constantly tended by worker bees.

Drones are male bees whose only task is to mate with the queen. There are only a few of them in the hive, and at the end of every summer they are turned out to die in the cold of winter. If they stayed in the hive, they would eat too much and do nothing in return.

Finally there are thousands of *workers*. Worker bees are sterile females. It is their role to perform all the tasks that need to be done around the hive – they look after the queen and the eggs that she lays; they make the hexagonal cells in which the eggs are laid and food stored; they guard the hive against robber bees, and keep it cool if necessary by fanning their wings; they collect the hive's food. Honey is made from the nectar that bees collect from flowers, and since such a lot is needed to support the hive over the winter, workers are constantly on the lookout over the summer for new clumps of flowers. When they have spotted some, they return to the hive and relay the message to other workers who will go out and collect the nectar.

The language of bees is extremely complicated, and much of it has been dis-

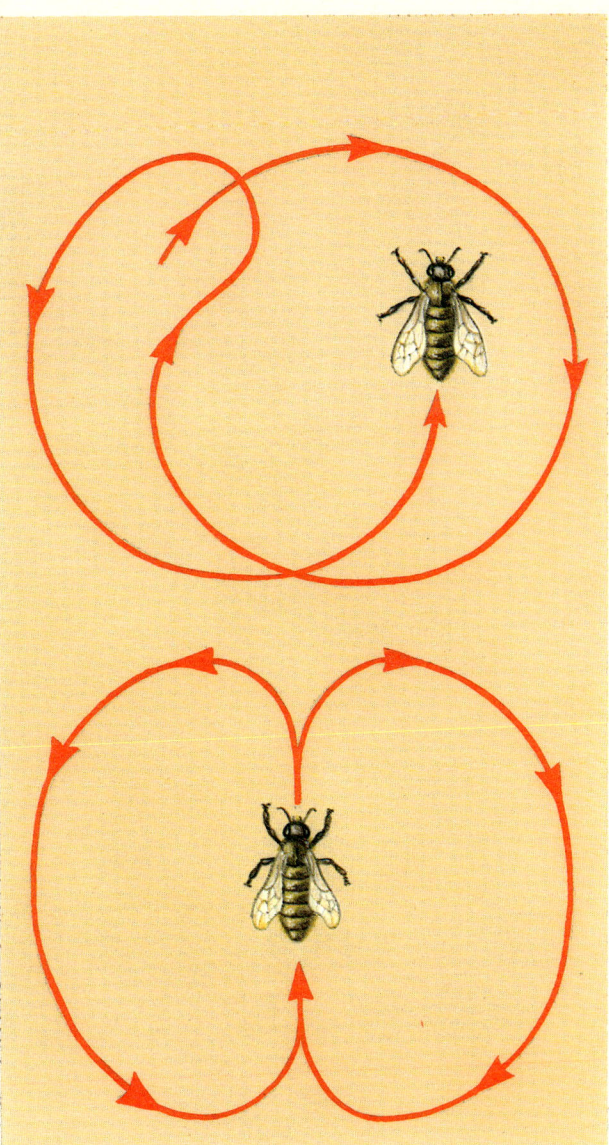

Wasps are unlike bees in a number of ways, although it is sometimes not easy to tell them apart. To begin with, not all wasps live in colonies and their nests are not made of wax, as the honey bees' are. Instead, they use a substance called 'carton', a papery material made of chewed wood, but they also have many similarities. Once again the nest is divided into social layers – the queen, the drones and the workers, and the wasps usually feed on nectar like the bees do, although they do not make honey.

covered through filming bees' activities. The language takes the form of dances, each one meaning a different thing. The scout bee dances perhaps in a figure-of-eight; if the dance is smooth and 'round' the nectar is quite near, if the tail is 'wagged' then it is further away. There are also signs that tell the nectar gatherers which direction in which to fly, and so on.

When the eggs hatch, each larva is fed on a special brood-food, 'royal jelly', made by the workers. If a new queen is required, she will be fed on this royal jelly all the time; the others will be given honey and pollen after about three days, and they will be workers. When the new queen is adult, it is her task to fly off and mate and so the whole process begins again.

To look at, it is not too hard to tell a wasp from a bee. The wasp has the bright yellow and black stripes and the more pointed body, while the bee is more dull, with a blunted, quite furry body. However, never be tempted to touch a bee or a wasp. Both insects have a sting. In the case of the wasp, this can be very painful indeed, and in the case of the bee, it will be painful not only to you but to the bee too, as stinging you will kill it.

Fish

With 20,000 species, fish make up one of the largest groups of animals on the earth, and each one is different from the rest. But it is possible to divide the fish world up very simply into a number of categories – those that live in fresh or salt water, those with a bone skeleton or a gristle one, and those which eat plankton and algae and those which eat meat.

Take sharks, for example. Sharks live in salt water and like their relatives, the rays, their skeletons are made of gristle. There are many kinds of sharks, some of them eating plankton while others eat meat, but perhaps the oddest of them to look at is the Hammerhead shark. This strange creature's head is not shaped like any other fish's. Instead it grows out sideways, with one eye at the end of each side, giving it a most peculiar expression!

Quite a different sort of fish is the seahorse. This tiny creature swims upright in the water, and its head with its long snout looks not unlike a horse. The seahorse's tail is useful too, in that it can be hooked like a finger around seaweed or rock to hold the fish steady in the water.

The next time you eat plaice or sole, look at the shape of the fish very carefully. It's flat, isn't it? Well, it may seem odd, but it didn't start out like that. When plaice or any of the flatfish hatch, they look exactly like any other fish. But as they grow older, a startling change occurs. They begin to tilt over until they swim on their side. As they start to tilt, the eye on the lower side of the body moves round and up until both eyes are on the same side of the head. This is done for a very good reason – flatfish tend to stay on the seabed. With both eyes on top of the head, they can see everything that is going on around them, instead of having one eye face down in the sand.

In the deeper parts of the ocean some of the most mysterious fish are found. One of these is the deep sea angler fish. The angler shares an exciting skill with such creatures as glow-worms – it can create its own light. As you can see from the picture, the angler has a long fishing-rod-like organ hanging over its large mouth. As it swims around in the darkness of the deep sea, its prey are attracted to the glow, come to investigate, and find themselves eaten. The angler is not the only fish with this ability. Many of the deep sea fish have it, though not always solely for the purpose of catching their prey. Some fish have rows of luminous cells along their sides, perhaps to act as attractions for the opposite sex.

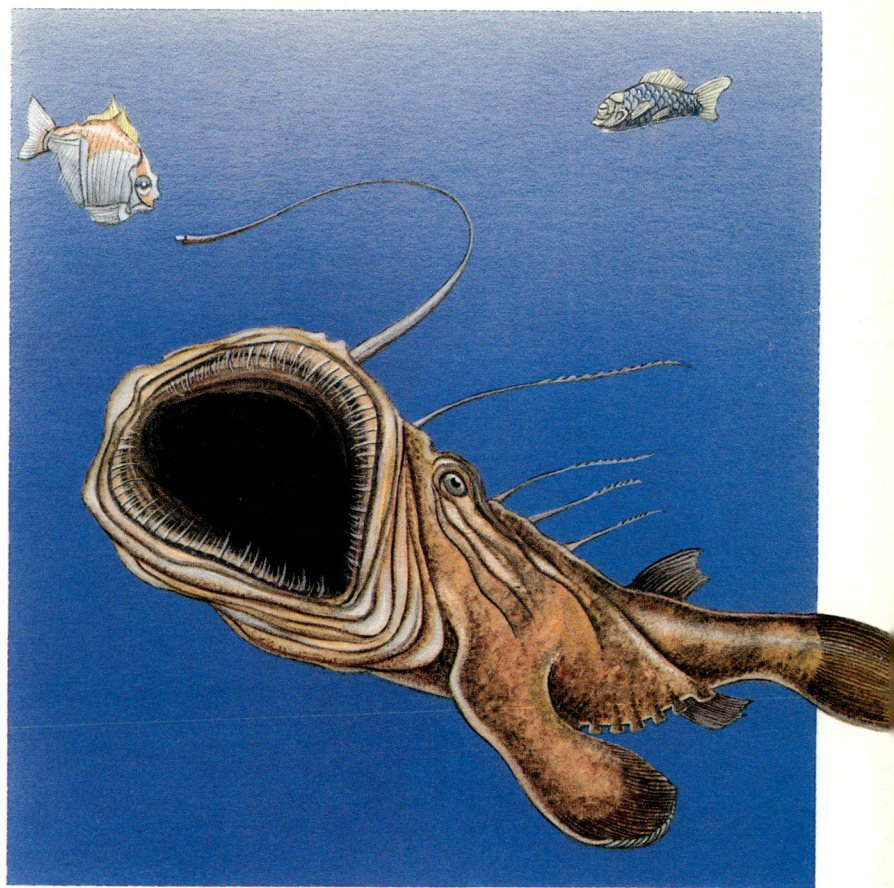

The warm seas contain many beautiful and interesting life forms, but perhaps the most beautiful is the coral which forms the Great Barrier Reef off the north-east coast of Australia. A reef is formed when many thousands of coral skeletons, in each of which the coral *polyp* lives, fuse together to form a large mass. The coral polyp is a relative of the sea anemone, but it creates a hard skeleton to protect its soft body from predators, and when alive and underwater, the colours of a reef are a constant delight to tourists.

Not only is the coral itself fascinating, but some of the animals which make their homes on the reef attract a great deal of attention, too.

One of these is the giant clam. The clam is a shellfish, which keeps the opening of its shell facing upwards. This is not because it catches fish as they swim past. Inside the shell, the soft part of the clam plays host to small green *algae* (tiny plants) which, like all green plants, can make their own food. The clam lives on this food, and keeps its shell open to let in the sunlight, but will close it again very quickly if anything should interfere with the algae. This means that swimmers must take great care not to touch the clams, as a foot trapped in deep water could mean trouble.

Amphibians

The life-cycle of the frog is one of the most interesting in the whole animal kingdom, as you will know if you have ever watched the development of the frog from tadpole to adult.

In the late spring, you can see in ponds and streams large clumps of jelly 'marbles', each containing a black speck. These are the eggs of the frog, usually called *spawn*, and there may be hundreds of them in one clump.

A frog's egg hardly shows any sign of life for several days. Then, at last, it begins to grow. By feeding on the yolk of its egg, it grows quite swiftly, developing a tail and gills. Finally it leaves the jelly of the egg, and begins to feed on plants. It is known now as a *tadpole*. The tadpole grows quickly, developing back legs and becoming stronger. It begins to eat meat rather than plants. Front legs appear, and the tadpole is obviously taking on a frog-

Frogs are often mistaken for toads, and in fact there is a great resemblance – but there are also big differences which should tell you at once what the animal is. To begin with, a frog has very smooth skin, whereas a toad is covered in small bumps or *warts*. The second difference is in the way frogs and toads move from place to place. A frog's back legs are long and very powerful, and it tends to jump or leap. A toad, on the other hand, has shorter back legs, and takes smaller leaps or merely crawls along. Finally, if you begin with spawn, you can tell at once whether the animal which hatches out will be a frog or a toad. Frogspawn is laid in clumps, whereas toadspawn is usually found in long necklaces, looped around plants.

Newts look very different from frogs and toads, and are sometimes mistaken for lizards. They have the same smooth skin as a frog, and their eggs are laid underwater, but not in clumps or necklaces. Instead the female lays her eggs one at a time under the leaves of pond plants. When the babies hatch out, they have no legs like other tadpoles, but they do have feathery gills before their lungs are developed.

shape, apart from its long tail. As the tail becomes shorter, so the rest of the tadpole's body develops – it now has lungs instead of gills for breathing, and finally can emerge from the water and live on land, although frogs prefer damp places.

Animals whose life-cycle is like that of the frog – who are born and develop in water and later can also live on land – are called amphibians, and include toads and newts.

Amphibians are what is called *cold-blooded* creatures. This means that their body temperature rises and falls as their surroundings change. During the winter, amphibians would freeze to death if they remained active and awake, so they *hibernate*. This long sleep carries on throughout the winter months – frogs sometimes bury themselves under the mud at the bottom of the pond, while newts often curl up under stones.

Reptiles

A reptile is an animal that has dry, scaly skin, is cold-blooded, and lays eggs rather than giving birth to live young. Snakes, crocodiles, lizards and tortoises belong to the reptile family, although at first glance they may bear little resemblance to each other.

Snakes such as the cobra are sometimes kept by snake charmers. Rearing up when their basket is opened, they sway from side to side in time to the charmer's music, and appear to dance. In fact, the snake is only following the movements of the charmer – it cannot hear the music.

Snakes

Snakes are arguably the most interesting of the reptiles, though they have by far the worst reputation. The majority of snakes are not venomous, and most are shy creatures which avoid humans wherever possible and strike only as a last resort. Despite this, many strange tales are told about snakes and their activities. One of the most common – and silly – is that the snake's flickering forked tongue will sting you. This is nonsense. No snake stings and the harmless tongue is used only as an aid to the snake's sense of smell.

In the case of venomous snakes, the bite is given by a set of fangs in the snake's mouth, each of which has a duct or channel down its centre or one side, along which the venom may travel from a gland.

Many snakes, including pythons and boas, kill by *constriction*, throwing their coils around the prey – usually a small mammal – and squeezing until the animal dies from suffocation. When it is dead, the prey is swallowed whole. Other snakes eat nothing but eggs, swallowing them whole, breaking them open inside the body, and ejecting the shell.

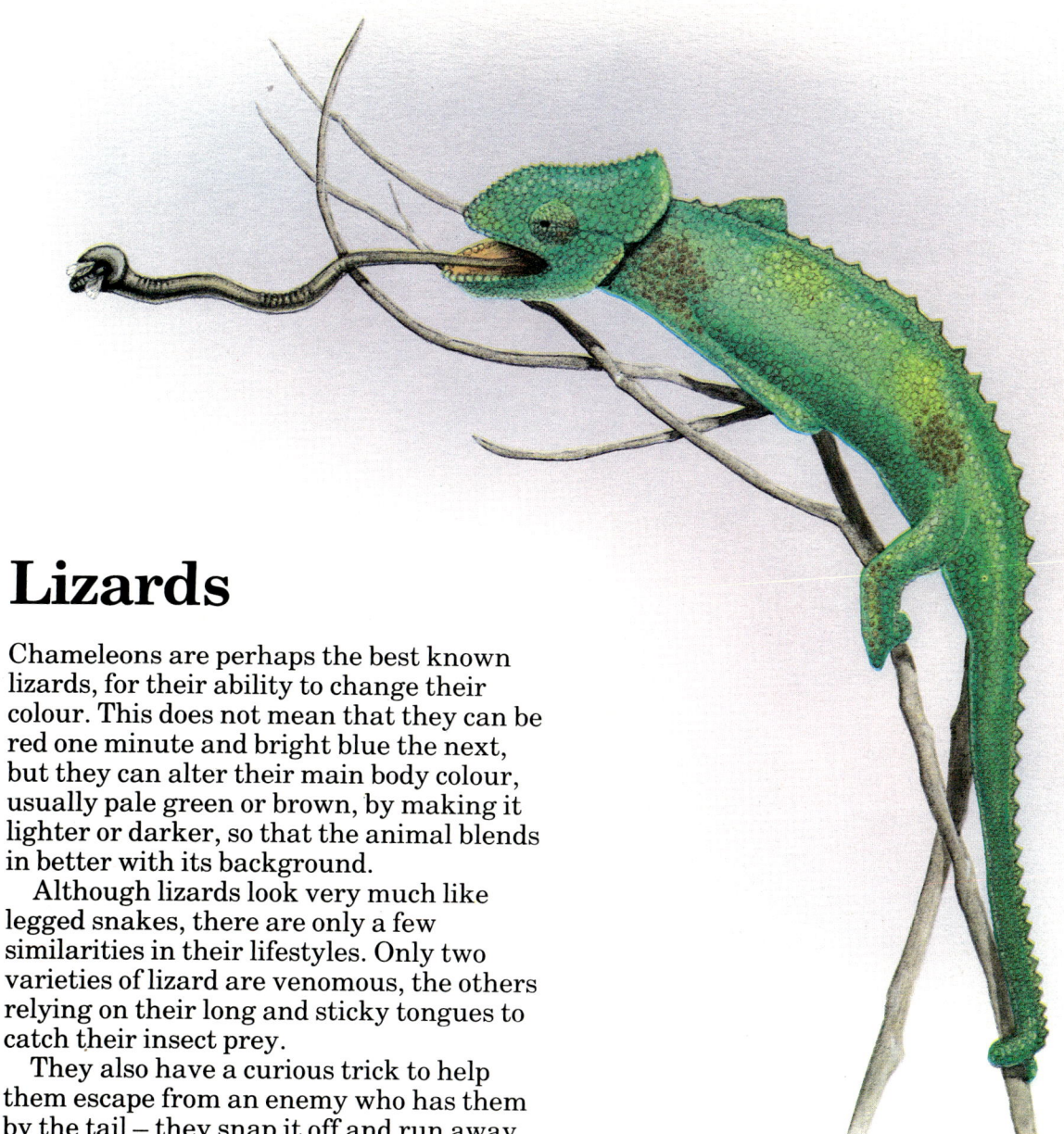

Lizards

Chameleons are perhaps the best known lizards, for their ability to change their colour. This does not mean that they can be red one minute and bright blue the next, but they can alter their main body colour, usually pale green or brown, by making it lighter or darker, so that the animal blends in better with its background.

Although lizards look very much like legged snakes, there are only a few similarities in their lifestyles. Only two varieties of lizard are venomous, the others relying on their long and sticky tongues to catch their insect prey.

They also have a curious trick to help them escape from an enemy who has them by the tail – they snap it off and run away to fight another day. After a while, a new tail grows.

Crocodiles and alligators are very like large lizards in appearance. Being river animals, their eyes, ears and nostrils are on top of their heads, and they have fierce teeth to deal with their prey of fish, frogs and often larger animals. Crocodiles are also very well protected by their armoured skin and heavy tails.

The beak of the northern Bald Eagle, showing its great strength.

Birds

How do you tell if a creature is a bird? Simple – if it has feathers, then it is a bird. Every bird has a number of different sorts of feathers, some for flying, some for body warmth, and some for display to attract a mate. Birds spend a good deal of time *preening* their feathers – which means that they clean them with their beak and comb them back into place. They will also make them waterproof, using oil from a gland near the tail.

Food

Birds eat a great variety of things, ranging from the small mammals caught by eagles and hawks to the insects eaten by smaller birds. Many others eat seeds and nuts, and the hummingbirds of America live on the nectar from flowers, as do bees. It is usually possible to tell what sort of food a bird eats by the shape of its beak. A seed-eating finch, for example, has a short, rather pointed bill, while an insect-eating swallow's beak is longer and thinner and more suited to catching its prey on the wing. Carnivorous birds such as the eagles, hawks and vultures have strong curved beaks designed for tearing and cutting.

What the bird eats depends very much on its habitat and surrounding weather conditions, and these factors also have a great effect on the migratory habits of birds, too.

This European Greenfinch has a short, conical bill, which tells us that it is a seed-eater.

The hummingbird hovers while reaching for its diet of nectar with its long bill.

Migration

Perhaps one of the best known European migrants is the swallow. It arrives in Europe in April or May, stays until the weather becomes cooler once again, and then returns south to warmer African countries. The reason for this is simply to do with the swallow's diet. Eating insects, caught mostly on the wing, the swallow needs a constant supply of food; when the food itself dies off in the cool months of the European autumn, the swallow must go south to warmer weather to avoid starvation.

There are migrating birds all over the world. In the Southern Hemisphere they will fly north, and in the Northern Hemisphere south, towards the warmer weather round the equator.

How do the birds find their way to and from these warmer countries? Not very much is known about this, but it is believed that they rely for steering on the position of the sun and stars, much as sailors used to do. Unlike sailors, however, no instruments are needed, as the ability to fly to a warm winter home is inborn in migrating birds.

The Baya weaver bird and its amazing nest, woven in this spectacular shape to keep snakes away from the eggs. Like every other nest-builder, the skill is inborn, and the weaver bird needs no teaching.

All birds lay eggs, and the majority of them build nests in which they can incubate them. Small birds such as blackbirds and thrushes build nests in traditional dish shapes, made with twigs and grass and lined with moss and feathers. Larger birds such as pigeons and crows, whose nests are often found in trees rather than hedges, make their nests of sticks and twigs. Swallows and swifts build nests of mud under the eaves of barns and houses. These are usually cup-shaped, while the nests of woodpeckers can be found hidden in holes in the trunks of trees.

Large and Flightless Birds

The ostrich is one of the most peculiar-looking birds in the world, and one of the very few that cannot fly. To make up for this, the ostrich's legs have become extremely long and powerful, enabling it to escape predators by running quickly away, and the two small wings it still has help it to keep its balance.

The penguin has similarly adapted to cope with a flightless life. Its wings are used for swimming, and have become more like flippers than wings. The bird's body too has altered, becoming thicker and fatter to deal with the extreme cold of its Antarctic home. The penguin's swimming is aided by the streamlined shape of its body, and by the fact that its feathers are very short, so that they resemble fur, to cut down on water resistance.

Birds of Prey

Although many carnivorous birds eat insects and grubs, there are many which catch and eat small mammals, and others whose food consists of animals killed by some other animal. These birds are

Many larger birds live near water, either fresh or sea water. Herons are typical waterside birds, and can often be seen standing motionless on their long legs in shallow water, waiting for a fish to come close enough. Herons, like other fish-eaters, have long necks and beaks, although the neck is curved back during flight, to form a graceful S shape.

Also in fresh water live ducks, swans and geese, whose diet consists chiefly of molluscs, plants and fishes, but who will eat practically anything. Ducks have developed webbed feet to enable them to paddle around, and their beaks are wide and flat, to cope with feeding in the water.

Seabirds tend to eat more fish than anything else. Gulls are perhaps the best-known, although there are many other species which compete with them for food.

One of the most spectacular of the seabirds is the cormorant, which catches its fish by means of a death-defying dive into the sea, followed by a swift ascent, with the prey in its beak, to the cliff top. Most seabirds nest on cliffs, their eggs being sharply pointed at one end to ensure that if pushed, they will spin round in a circle rather than roll off the edge.

known as birds of prey, and are among the most interesting.

The buzzard, falcon and sparrowhawk are all birds of prey, and are adapted in a number of ways to this life. The eyesight of these birds is very good indeed, and sometimes the sense of smell is too, as their prey – which may be just a mouse in a field – is often tiny. The beaks of such birds are, as would be expected, very strong and curved, to enable them to tear flesh and fur, and the feet too have great strength.

Scavengers (birds which eat dead meat) also have great strength in their beaks and claws, since their prey may be something as tough as a buffalo. Vultures and condors belong to this group, and the bald necks and heads of the vultures make them one of the least attractive birds.

Rodents

The word *rodent* means *gnawing animal*, and that is what all rodents are, from the smallest shrew to the largest rodent of all, the capybara. Each rodent has a pair of long curving incisor teeth in each jaw, and these stick out at the front of the mouth, giving a very strong family resemblance. These teeth are remarkable in that they do not stop growing, and to avoid them becoming too long and potentially dangerous, the rodent must gnaw things such as wood and even metal to wear down the teeth.

Most rodent young are born blind and helpless, with the exception of the guinea pigs and coypus, which can forage for themselves soon after birth. The fur appears later, and many rodents are well known for their coats. Especially sought after is the chinchilla, a small wild rodent which has the softest, thickest fur in the animal kingdom, but beaver, squirrel and musk rat (or musquash) are also considered valuable.

Rats and mice are perhaps the best-known rodents, being more likely to share the habitat of humans. House mice are very common, and rats are second only to insects in their spreading of disease among the human population of the world – the fleas carried by the black rat *(rattus rattus)* were responsible for several outbreaks of plague in the middle ages and the seventeenth century.

However there are many rodents whose docility makes them very popular as pets – guinea pigs and hamsters, for example. Another rodent which many humans find endearing is the squirrel, although many farmers and agriculturalists regard it as a pest.

The Beaver - the Great Engineer

The beaver is one of the largest rodents, and also one of the greatest construction engineers in the animal kingdom. Using only teeth and hands for tools, and wood for material, the beaver can build canals, dams and lodges. Dams in particular are skilled constructions – where the current of the river to be dammed is strong, the dam itself is built on a curve ideal to withstand the pressure, showing the beaver's inborn understanding of stress and strain forces. The use of trees both as building material and as food – beavers eat bark – means that in certain parts of the world it is regarded as a pest. But in others, where trees have been cut down for use by humans, the beaver could soon be in danger of dying out.

The Suicidal Lemming

The Scandinavian Lemming is one of the most interesting of all the rodents and has long provided a talking point amongst biologists. Roughly every third or fourth year, the lemming populations experience something close to panic, and all begin a mass migration.

In Scandinavia, the migrations always start from one of five different centres, and they always proceed in the same directions. The initial cause seems to be overpopulation and lack of food as a result, but it has been noticed that the lemmings will not stop in their frantic migration even if the route takes them through fertile country. Neither do they stop at the coast, but will swim until exhaustion overtakes them and drowning follows.

This migration becomes still more interesting when it is realised that every year this happens, other animals are experiencing something similar – 'lemming years' are years when certain butterfly caterpillars are so numerous that they can strip forests bare, and when certain types of shrew also migrate, although not to the same extent.

Herd Animals and Predators

On the great plains of Africa are found many sorts of animal which live in herds. The best known of these animals are possibly various types of antelope, who would be almost completely defenceless if they lived on their own or in pairs. In their case there is safety in numbers.

The main predators of antelopes are the big cats, lions and cheetahs, who have the stamina to chase for some time. Antelopes can run quite fast, but they have not the strength to keep up their speeds for very long. Therefore, it helps to keep closely together in a large bunch, so that it isn't so easy for the lion or cheetah to single out one animal and concentrate on chasing that one. Of course, there are occasions when this doesn't work and one animal does get separated from the rest of the herd. In this case, the others will sacrifice it for the good of the rest of them.

Antelopes are extremely graceful creatures which eat mainly grass and low-growing plants, although some – for example the gerenuk – have long legs and necks and can reach quite high. All antelopes have horns, ranging from the great curved horns of the sable antelope to the short ones of the little dik-diks.

Among some of the more unpleasant animals of the plains are the hyenas. They are about the size of a large dog, with a sloping back and a short mane down the ridge of it. Hyenas do kill their own prey, but more often than not they rely on there being a carcase left on the plain by a lion or cheetah. The hyena's cry is a most peculiar sound. It is given when food is found, and sounds very like a human laughing. During the day, hyenas tend to rest in burrows or amongst rocks. They roam the plains in large packs.

The Larger Mammals

The African elephant is the largest land mammal in the world, being slightly larger than the Indian one. African elephants live in grass and woodlands, and despite their great size are usually placid creatures. The elephant's trunk – one of the strangest features of any mammal – is an extemely long nose, which is very useful for collecting food and water, and for sniffing the air for the scent of other animals.

Taller than the elephant, though by no means as bulky, is the giraffe. Found only in Africa, the giraffe is a neighbour of the elephant, and its long neck enables it to reach its leaf-food high above the heads of other animals. But that long neck is something of a problem when it comes to drinking. A giraffe cannot bend its neck and so it must stand with its front legs splayed wide, which brings its neck and head closer to the water.

One of the strangest of all mammals is the kangaroo of Australia. The kangaroo has extemely powerful back legs which enable it to jump rather than walk as other mammals do, its tail helping it to balance. Baby kangaroos are only about 1 inch (3 cm) long when they are born, and immediately make their way to the mother's pouch, where they grow until they are old enough to look after themselves. Kangaroos belong to a type of mammal called *marsupial*, a word which means *pouched animal*.

Unlike many of the large mammals, bears are carnivores, eating fish and smaller mammals as well as nuts, leaves and roots. Some bears can grow to be about 10 feet (3 metres) long, weighing about 300 pounds (145 kg). Some sorts of bear, for example the Grizzly bear of America, are dangerous animals and have been known to attack and kill human beings, but other bears like American Black bears will only attack when they are wounded or looking after their young. Young bears are born helpless and blind, but they grow quickly and are mature after about two years.

Related to the bears is the giant panda, a great favourite at zoos. In the wild the panda lives in China and Tibet, and feeds on young bamboo. There are very few pandas left now, and so attempts are being made to breed pandas in captivity. Very few successes have been achieved, despite expert scientific advice.

The Big Cats

If you compare a fully-grown lion or tiger with an adult domestic cat, the first difference you will notice is that of size. An adult lion can reach a length of over seven feet (2.5 metres), and a Siberian tiger can be over ten feet (3 metres) from nose to tip of tail. But there are a good many similarities, both in the habits of the big cats and in their physical resemblance to the smaller domestic breeds.

The big cats, like the domestic ones, are carnivorous — that is, they eat meat — but unlike them, the lion and the tiger will eat quite large mammals such as antelope, zebra and even buffalo.

The big cats are fast and extremely strong, the cheetah taking the speed record of up to 70 miles (113km) an hour for short distances. This enables it to catch and kill any of the antelope of the African grasslands, which are its prey.

The lion is much larger than the cheetah, and has earned the nick-name *king of the beasts* because of the majestic appearance of the male lion. Lions live in small groups called *prides,* consisting of one or two males and several lionesses and their cubs. It is the lionesses which do the hunting for food; the males eat first, but would quickly starve if they had to fend for themselves.

Tigers are also big cats, but they live in Asia, and some are found in quite cold regions. Unlike the average domestic cat, tigers are quite at home in water, and a good deal of their food consists of fish they have caught. Young elephants are sometimes in danger from them, as tigers will eat up to sixty pounds (about 26 kg) of meat a night. Because we more often than not see a tiger in a zoo, we do not appreciate the effectiveness of its camouflaging stripes. But seen in its usual setting of thick leaves and reeds, the tiger is extemely well hidden.

Although the great majority of big cats live in Africa and Asia, there are a few which live in northern Europe. Perhaps the best-known of these is the lynx, which is also found in Siberia, and in Canada. The lynx looks even more like a domestic cat than a lion, although there are differences. It has longer legs, for example, large paws to enable it to travel over snow, and tufts of hair on its ears. It is about the size of a large dog, and has been known to kill and eat small deer and domestic sheep and goats.

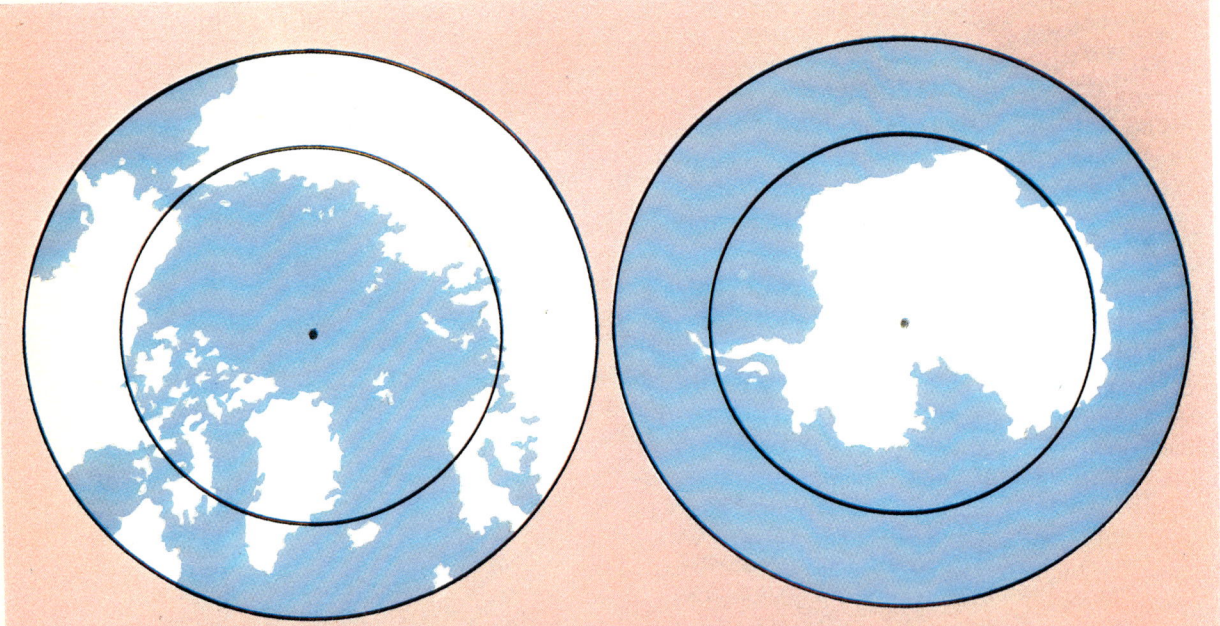

The Polar Regions

The Arctic is the name given to the area round the North Pole, and consists almost entirely of the Arctic Ocean, whose 3½ million square miles (9 million square kilometres) is almost completely covered with a permanent icepack. The Arctic Circle, which includes the northernmost tips of Asia, Canada and Europe, as well as almost all of Greenland, is surprisingly well-populated, with Eskimos in Alaska, Canada and Greenland, and Lapps in northern Norway, Sweden and Finland.

The Antarctic is the continent around the South Pole, and is made up of 5 million square miles (13 million square kilometres) of land covered with a thick layer of ice more than 9000 feet (2700 metres) deep. Life can only exist round the coastal regions, and then it is only animals which can support themselves in the extreme cold.

The animals of the Arctic region include the polar bear, walruses and seals, and the snowy owl, while in Antarctica are found penguins and the huge Blue whale.

The polar bear is one of the largest bears, and is a meat-eater, its prey being mostly seals. Being white, the polar bear is not easy to spot in its icy surroundings, and its tremendous speed across the snow is another of the advantages it has over its prey.

Seals have a layer of tough, spongy tissue filled with an oily fat just under the surface of their skin, to protect them from the extreme cold. They are excellent swimmers, able to stay under water for up to half an hour. Walruses look rather like seals, except that they are much bigger – reaching lengths of up to ten feet (3.5 metres) and weights of up to 3000 pounds (1300 kg) – and they have long tusks, sometimes as long as 30 inches (75cm) which project downwards from the upper jaw.

The Blue whale is the largest living animal in the world. Like other whales, it is in fact a mammal, breathing air, and would drown if it did not come up to the surface every five or ten minutes. Baby whales are born in the sea, but coaxed quickly to the surface for air, and like other mammals they are fed on mother's milk. Despite its great size, the Blue whale eats *plankton,* microscopically small sea plants and animals, which it takes in through its mouth, filters, then squeezes out the water with its tongue. It is by no means a vicious animal, but will attack if wounded or frightened.

Monkeys and Apes

Monkeys, apes and humans are all related to one another, as you will have noticed if you have ever watched the expressions change on a chimpanzee's face or seen the way a monkey can use its hands as tools like a human.

Apes, including the chimpanzee, the gorilla and the orang-utan, are the closest relatives of humans, and tend to spend most of their time in the safety of trees, coming down to ground level to feed.

The gorilla, despite its great size and frightening appearance, is a gentle creature unless it is molested or attacked, but it has not gained the popularity of the chimpanzee, possibly because it is slow to learn tricks and does not have the endearing face of its smaller relative.

The chimpanzee is a great favourite with humans, perhaps because it has so many human similarities. When a baby chimp is born, for example, it is cared for by its mother in almost exactly the same way as a human baby. There have even been incidents recorded of chimpanzees giving first aid to one another – a captive female was once seen to go whimpering to her mate who, after a close inspection of the cause of the trouble, gently picked out a piece of grit from her eye. It is not unusual, in fact, for wild chimpanzees to greet each other with that most human of gestures, a kiss.

The Rhesus monkey, although endearing, does not have the same human expression as the chimpanzee or the orangutan.

Monkeys differ from apes in that they are smaller, many have long tails, and they do not bear the same resemblance to humans. But both apes and monkeys belong to the family of mammals called *primates*. Both apes and monkeys are extremely intelligent, although their brains are not as highly developed as that of humans.

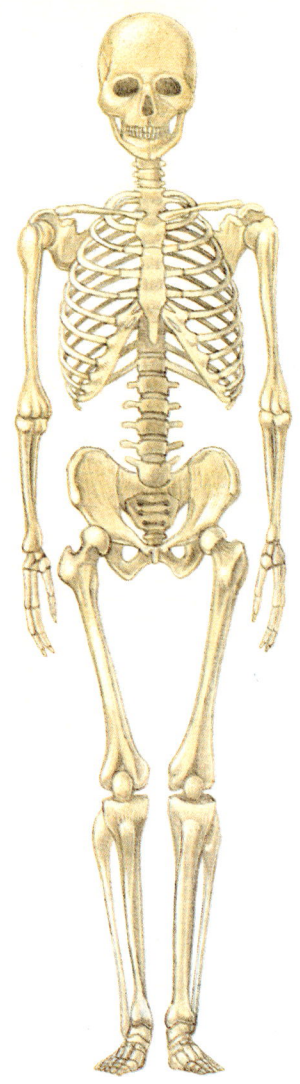

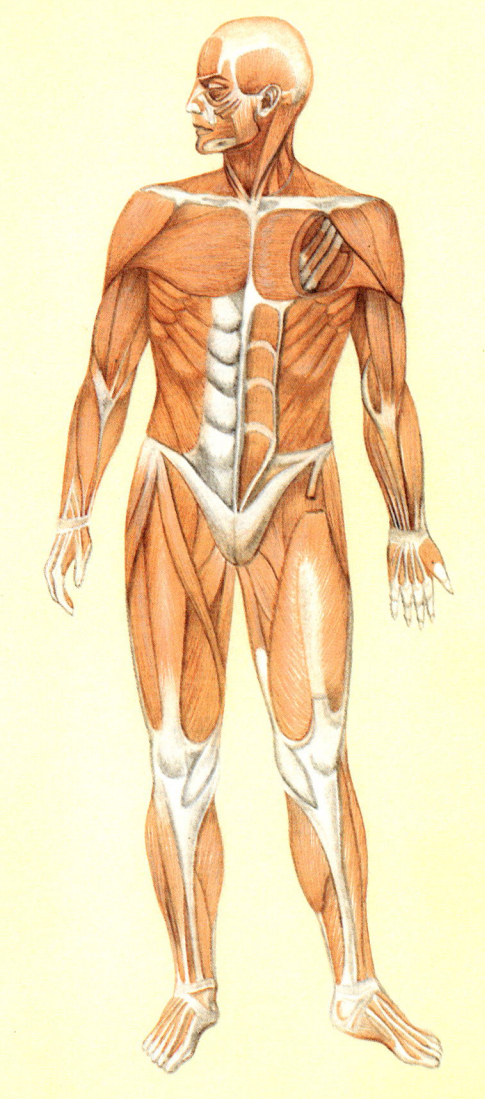

There are muscles over almost all your body, divided into three main types.

The most important muscle you have is the *cardiac muscle* in your heart, which keeps your heart beating. It can never be allowed to become tired, so it must be extemely strong to carry on working non-stop all the time.

The second type is the *involuntary muscle.* You have no control over the working of these muscles, as they control things like the movements of your stomach, intestines and blood vessels. You cannot feel them working either, so for most of the time you are not conscious of their presence.

The final type of muscle is the *voluntary muscle.* You have many of these, as they are the ones which we control to make, for example, our arms and legs do

The Human Body

Every human body is made up in exactly the same way, with a *skeleton, muscles, skin* and *hair*. Your skeleton is the framework of bones that keeps you upright, refusing to allow you to sag into a heap, and which protects the delicate and important organs of your body. When you are adult, you will have 206 bones in your skeleton; when you were born you had 270. As you grow, not only do your bones grow larger, but some of the smaller ones fuse together to give you greater strength. But your skeleton, though strong, would be of little use to you if you had no muscles to make it move in the direction and position you want it to.

what we want them to do. These muscles can become tired very easily, and need a good deal of rest. When you relax, these are the muscles which rest, while the other two carry on working.

Your skin is remarkable. It fits you perfectly, acting as a tight bag for your flesh, keeps repairing itself and replacing dead skin even though you do not notice it, and protects your delicate organs from harsh conditions and serious damage. It also helps regulate your body temperature by allowing excess heat to escape through it in the form of sweat, and warming you up by trapping heat in the 'goose-pimples' you can see when you feel cold. What is more, your hair and fingernails grow from it.

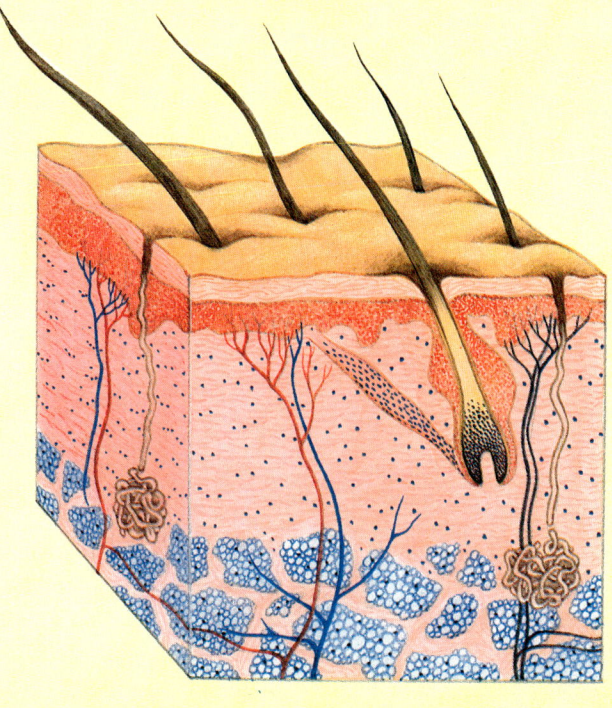

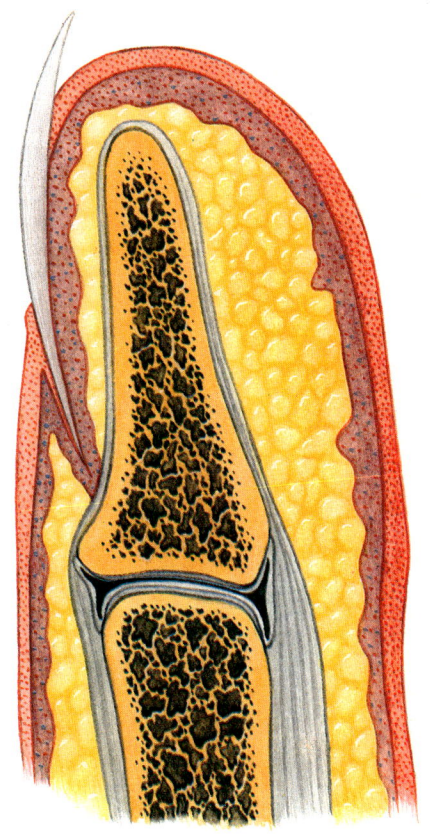

Compared to our closest relatives, the apes, we have very little hair. This is because we rely on our clothes, not our hair or fur, for warmth, so the greater part of our body hair has become very fine. We still have hair on our heads, however, because the body loses a lot of heat through the head; hair is a form of insulation.

We also have fingernails and toenails, which are the human equivalent of claws in the animal kingdom. Since we use tools and have no need for claws, our nails have become much smaller and softer. Both the hair and nails are made by cells in the skin. When they emerge so that we can see them, the cells which form them are dead. This is why it does not hurt you when you cut your fingernails or hair.

The Major Organs of the Human Body

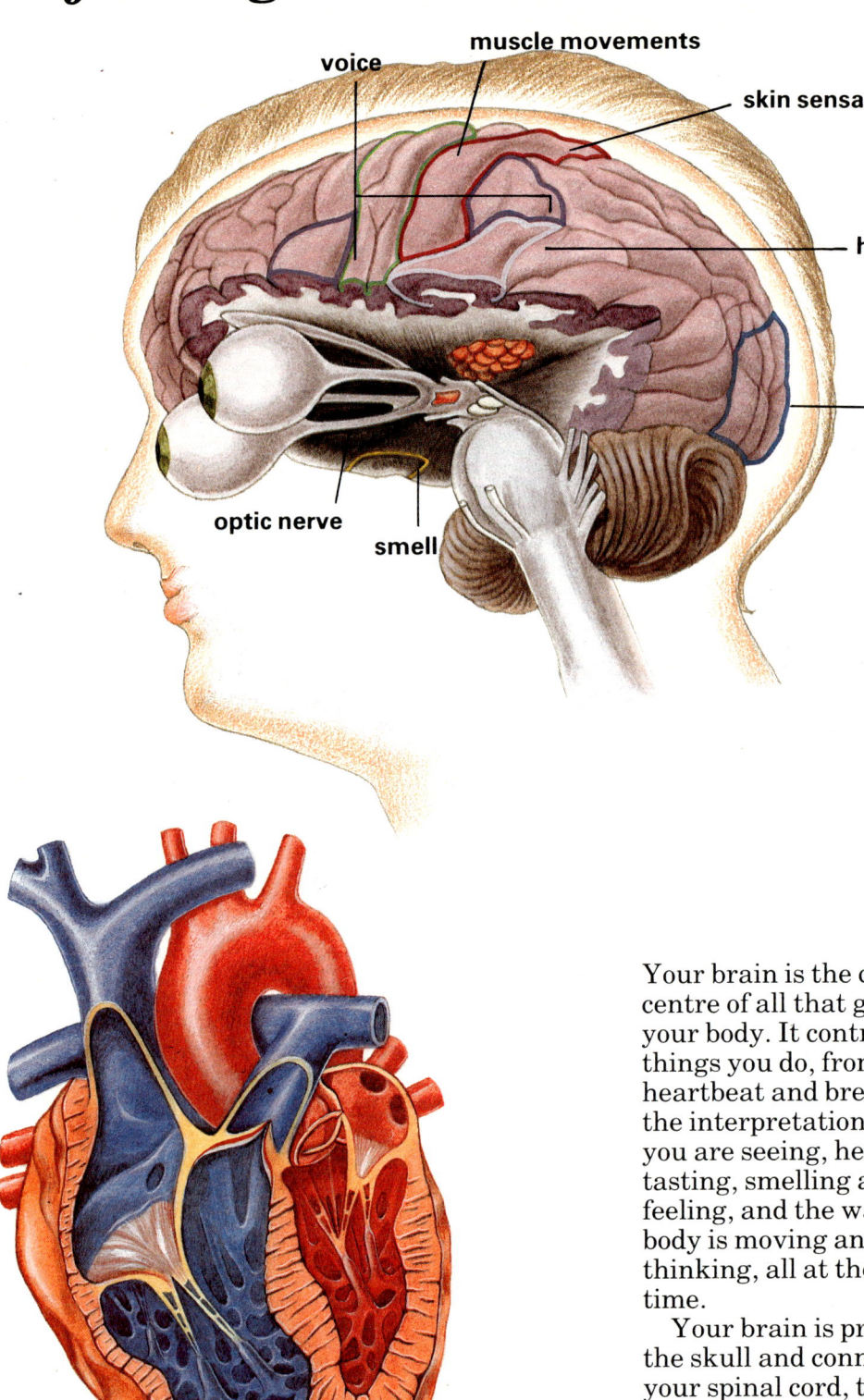

Your brain is the control centre of all that goes on in your body. It controls all the things you do, from your heartbeat and breathing, to the interpretation of what you are seeing, hearing, tasting, smelling and feeling, and the way your body is moving and thinking, all at the same time.

Your brain is protected by the skull and connected to your spinal cord, through which it can send messages to all parts of your body. Each part of the brain controls a different part of your body, as you can see from the diagram, and so it is vital that no part of it should become damaged. Unfortunately, this does happen sometimes, when for example a blood clot may enter the brain, and a part of it may shut down for a time while repairs are carried out. Generally though the brain remains healthy and active – your control centre. Your heart is also a very important organ, protected by your ribs and your breast bone. This means that, contrary to popular belief, it is not found on the left hand side of your body, but is more central. The heart is like a bag of muscles with four compartments shut off from one another by valves, which will only open one way, preventing the flow of blood in the wrong direction. Blood returns to the heart when it has delivered oxygen to the cells of the body. As it passes through the vessels in the lungs it collects more oxygen, and then as the heart pumps, it goes round the system again with its valuable cargo. This process goes on until we die.

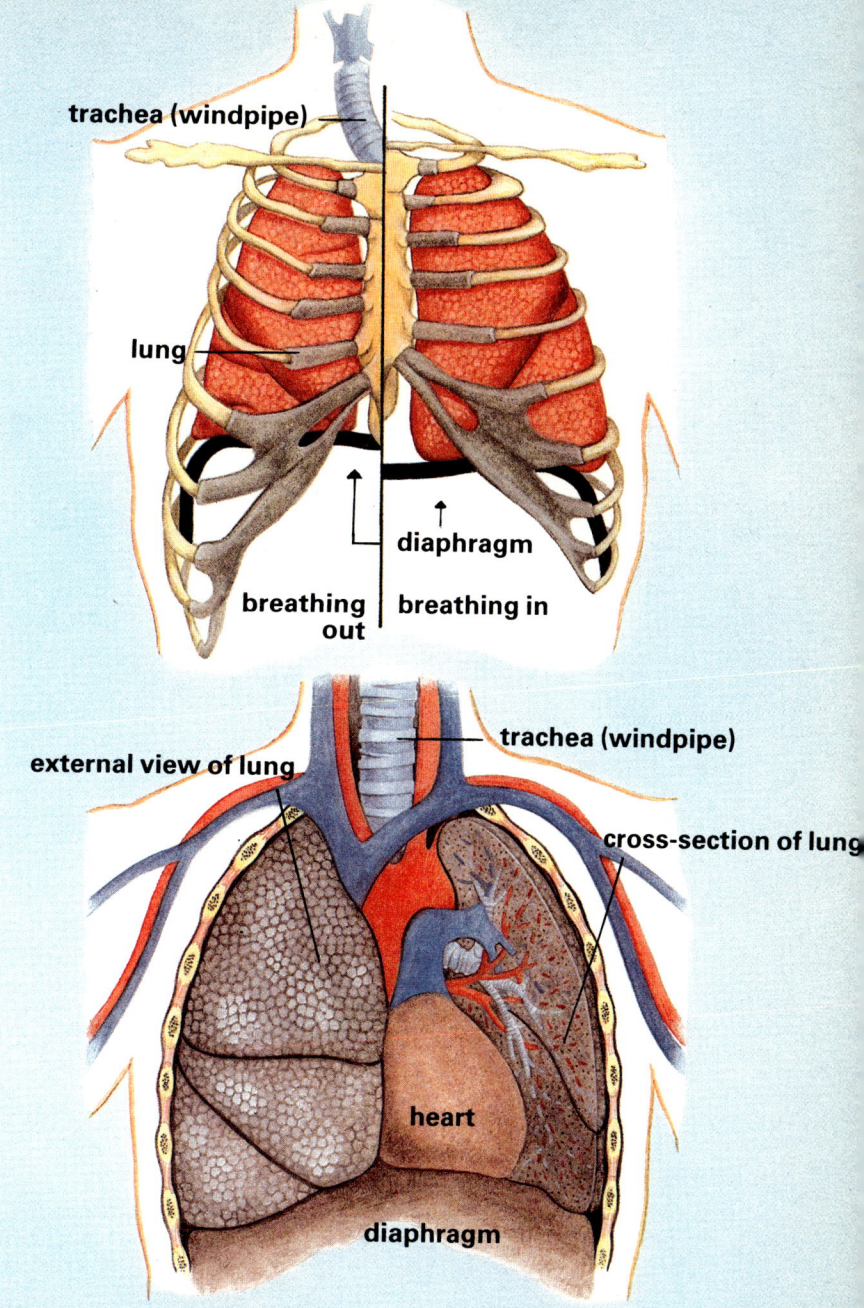

Everyone knows that the organs for breathing are the lungs. We need to breathe because otherwise we cannot convert the food we eat into energy – we need oxygen for this purpose, and we extract the oxygen from the air. Lungs will hold a large amount of air, although we do not often use our lungs to their full capacity. Inside, the lungs divide and redivide into lots of tiny air sacs, each one surrounded by blood vessels. As we breath, oxygen passes into these air sacs, taking carbon dioxide out of the blood vessels and replacing it. Carbon dioxide is poisonous to the body in large quantities, and we breathe it out into the air.

Because your lungs are so important, it is vital that they should not become infected, or have anything blocking them. For this reason, when our food 'goes down the wrong way', we start to cough until it is removed and we can breathe normally again.

The Five Senses

The Eye

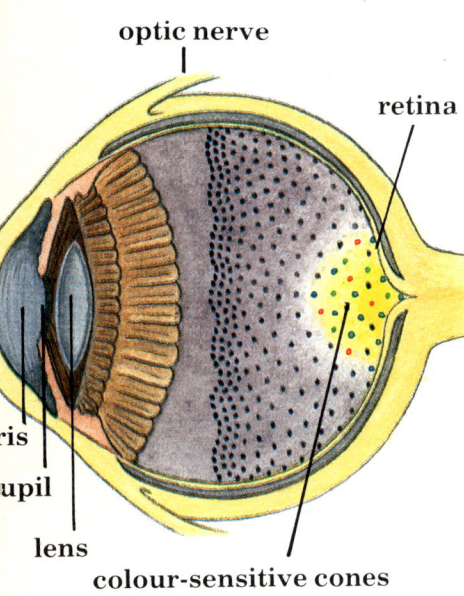

One of the most complex organs of the body, the eye's function is to collect messages in the form of light rays and transmit them to the brain for identification. Looking at the diagram, you can see that in the coloured *iris*, there is a hole called the *pupil*. This allows light into the eye, and contracts and expands as the amount of light varies. The *lens*, which also alters in shape to deal with the amount of light, focuses the image, which falls on to the *retina* at the back of the eye. Then the *optic nerve* takes the message of light waves to the brain for interpretation. Colour is perceived by special cells on the retina called *cones*, and colour blindness is the result if there should be a lack of a certain kind of cone – for example, those which detect the colour red.

People wear spectacles when the lens which focuses the image fails to do so, for one reason or another. In this case, an artificial lens is used by the optician to correct the fault and enable the person to see clearly again.

The Ear

The ear works on the principle that sound travels in vibrations, and it is the fleshy part of the ear, the *pinna*, which gathers and directs the vibrations into the *middle ear*. They travel along a passage to the *tympanic membrane* or ear drum, a tight skin over the passage which vibrates as the vibrations of sound hit it. Behind the ear drum are three tiny bones, the smallest bones in the body – the *malleus* (hammer), the *incus* (anvil) and the *stapes* (stirrup) – and they vibrate in turn. Behind them is a second membrane called the *oval window*, which leads to the *inner ear*.

By the time the vibrations reach this point, they are ready to be turned into impulses to be sent to the brain, and this job is done in the *cochlea*. This organ looks rather like a snail shell and contains nerve cells and fluid. The fluid moves as the vibrations strike it, and this triggers off a reaction in the nerve cells. Messages are sent along the nerve fibres, which join together to form the *auditory nerve*. This transmits the messages to the brain, where they are interpreted and identified.

The ear also contains the organs which control our sense of balance. As you can see from the diagram, in the inner ear there are three *semicircular canals*, each containing a sort of fluid with nerve cells floating in it. When your head is moving about, the fluid moves too and pushes the nerve cells. These send messages to the brain, which calculates the position of the head and compensates for the movement.

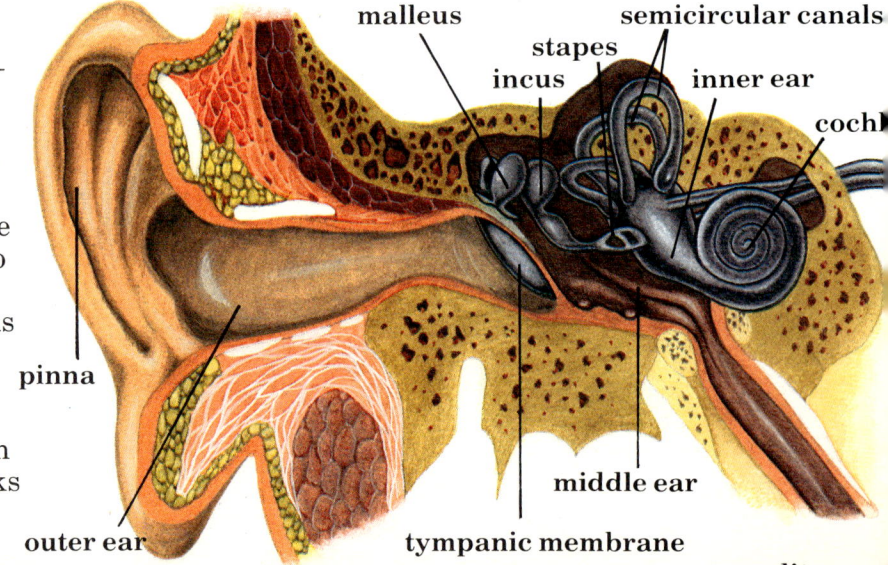

Touch

All over the surface of the human body there are nerve endings, connected to the *central nervous system* (CNS), which consists of the *brain* and the *spinal cord*. The nerve endings detect what goes on in the world outside the body, and send messages to the CNS about whatever comes into contact with it.

When something touches your skin, the nerve endings immediately send messages to the brain about how heavy the pressure is, whether the object touching you is hot or cold, soft or hard, and so on. The brain registers these and, providing there seems to be no danger, will allow you to go on touching whatever the object is.

But imagine that you touched a hot iron with your finger. The nerve endings in your finger would flash a 'too hot' message to a special nerve in the spinal cord. Immediately the message would return ordering the finger to move, and you would snatch your hand away. This happens so fast that you would not have time even to say 'ow', and you would not feel any pain until afterwards.

Pain is the body's warning system that something is wrong. Although we do not enjoy pain, we would be in grave danger without it, as we could do ourselves serious damage without being aware of it.

Taste and Smell

The two senses of taste and smell are very closely connected – in fact if your sense of smell is somehow impaired, for example by your having a cold, your sense of taste also seems to suffer.

Taste is detected by *taste buds* in your mouth, mostly on the upper surface of your tongue, but also on the roof of the mouth (the *palate*) and on the back of the throat. There are four types of taste bud – sweet, salt, sour and bitter – and everything we eat comes under one or other of these headings. In addition, our sense of smell adds to the flavour of what we eat.

We can detect many more smells than we can taste. Smells are carried to the nose in the air, and reach the smell or *olfactory cells* in the upper part of the nose. The olfactory cells are covered with a layer of *mucus,* in which the smell must be 'dissolved' before it can be detected. If you had a perfectly dry nose, you would be unable to smell. The olfactory cells are linked to nerve fibres, which send messages about the smells to the brain, which has a memory for them. Once you have smelled burning rubber, for example, you will easily recognise it again – but if you come across an unfamiliar smell you will not know what it is. In the same way, you will not be able to describe a smell like burning rubber to someone who has never experienced it for themselves!

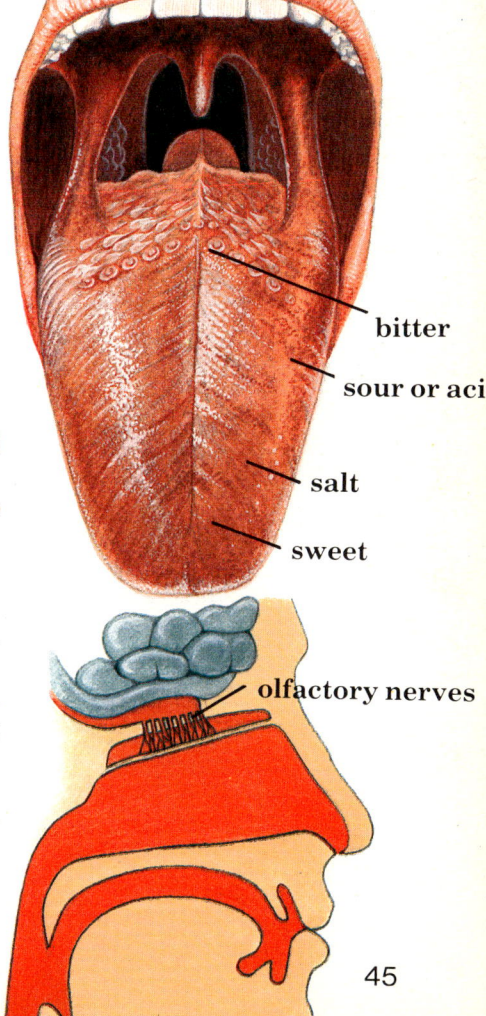

Glossary of Useful Terms: Plants

algae	are tiny plants which make their own food by photosynthesis.		which attracts insects to them and so helps pollination.
bark	covers the trunk and branches of trees as protection against harsh weather or damage.	**parasitic**	plants are those which, like fungi, cannot produce any of their own food, or, like mistletoe, can produce only some of it. By living off other things, they obtain the substances they need.
cambium	cells are the living cells which create the rings seen in the trunks of felled trees, and which help scientists to judge the age of trees.	**phloem**	cells carry the food of the tree or plant from the leaves, where it is made, to all other parts.
chlorophyll	is the green substance found in all green trees and plants which is essential for photosynthesis to take place.	**photo-synthesis**	is the process carried out by all green plants where sunlight, water, carbon dioxide and chlorophyll are used to make food.
cutin	is the waxy substance found on the needles of evergreen trees and on holly leaves, which prevents too much water escaping during cold weather and thus stops leaves falling.	**pollination**	is the transfer of pollen from the male part of the flower to the female part of the same or another flower, which results in the formation of seeds.
deciduous	trees are those which lose their leaves during cold weather.	**seeds**	are formed by all flowering plants. They contain almost all that is necessary to form new plants exactly the same as the parents.
evergreen	trees are those which keep their leaves throughout the winter.		
fungi	are plants which do not contain chlorophyll and therefore cannot manufacture their own food by photosynthesis.	**spores**	are the "seeds" of fungi, except that they are not formed by pollination since fungi have no flowers. Fungi do not need other fungi to produce spores, but can do it alone.
gills	are the parts of fungi below the cap which produce spores and enable the plants to reproduce.	**xylem**	cells are the hard woody cells found in trees and plants which carry water from the roots to all other parts.
nectar	is the sweet substance produced by flowering plants		

Glossary of Useful Terms: Animals

amphibians	are animals which can live and breathe in both water and air, most of them laying their eggs in water. They are cold-blooded.		poisonous in large quantities to oxygen-breathing animals. Carbon dioxide is present in the air, forming about 0.03% of it.
brain	The brain is the control centre of all vertebrates and some invertebrates. It controls everything from the heartbeat to the highly developed senses, and in intelligent animals such as humans, has the power to think and reason.	**carnivorous**	animals are those which eat meat, as opposed to grass and other vegetation.
		castes	are the 'classes' in colonies of social insects; in the case of bees there are three castes – the queen, the drones and the workers.
carbon dioxide	(CO_2) is a gas that plants need for photosynthesis, but is	**cell**	A cell contains all the information that is necessary about the living thing to which

	it belongs. In the case of single-celled animals, the cell also contains all the necessary organs to ensure life.	**omnivorous**	animals are those which, like most humans, eat both meat and vegetables.
central nervous system	In mammals and other vertebrates this consists of the brain and spinal cord, as opposed to all the other nerves in the body.	**oxygen**	is a gas that all breathing animals need to survive. It is given out by plants, and forms 20.9% of the air.
cold-blooded	or *poikilothermic* animals are those like reptiles and fishes whose body temperature varies according to the surroundings of the animal.	**peripheral nervous system**	This consists of all the nerves in the body apart from the brain and the spinal cord.
		plankton	are microscopic, often single-celled plants and animals usually found in water.
constriction	is a means by which certain snakes kill their prey, throwing coils round the victim and squeezing until the prey dies.	**primates**	are the highest and most advanced form of animal life, and include apes, monkeys and humans.
gills	are the breathing apparatus of those animals such as fish which do not have lungs. Water passes over the lungs, oxygen is extracted, and the water expelled.	**reptiles**	are cold-blooded, scaled animals who lay eggs instead of giving birth to live young.
		respiration	is the passage of oxygen to the cells of the body and the expelling of carbon dioxide.
herbivores	are those animals which eat only vegetation.	**rodents**	are mammals which gnaw.
hibernation	is the long winter sleep of certain small mammals, amphibians and snakes. It slows the body right down, so that energy is not used up when food is scarce.	**royal jelly**	is a specially nourishing substance made from nectar by bees, and fed to young bees.
		scavengers	are those animals which, like hyenas, feed upon the carcases of animals killed by others.
invertebrates	are animals which do not have backbones, such as insects.	**senses**	are the five ways by which animals discover what is happening around them. They are sight, hearing, touch, taste and smell.
mammals	are warm-blooded vertebrates which give birth to live young in most cases, suckle those young, and have body hair.	
marsupials	are pouched mammals, whose young are born extremely undeveloped, and must grow into adulthood in the parent's pouch.	**social insects**	are those which, like bees and ants, live together in colonies.
		spinal cord	is part of the central nervous system and is the main link between the peripheral nervous system and the brain.
mucus	is a thick liquid that lines the nasal and respiratory passages of mammals and which is essential for the sense of smell to function properly.	**vertebrates**	are those animals which have a backbone: birds, reptiles, amphibians, fishes and mammals.
nerves	are the means whereby vertebrates can discover what is happening around them. All nerves are connected to the brain.	**warm-blooded**	or *homothermic* animals, birds and mammals, are those whose body temperature is constant and does not vary according to their surroundings.